I Colored This Picture For You
by Donna Freitag

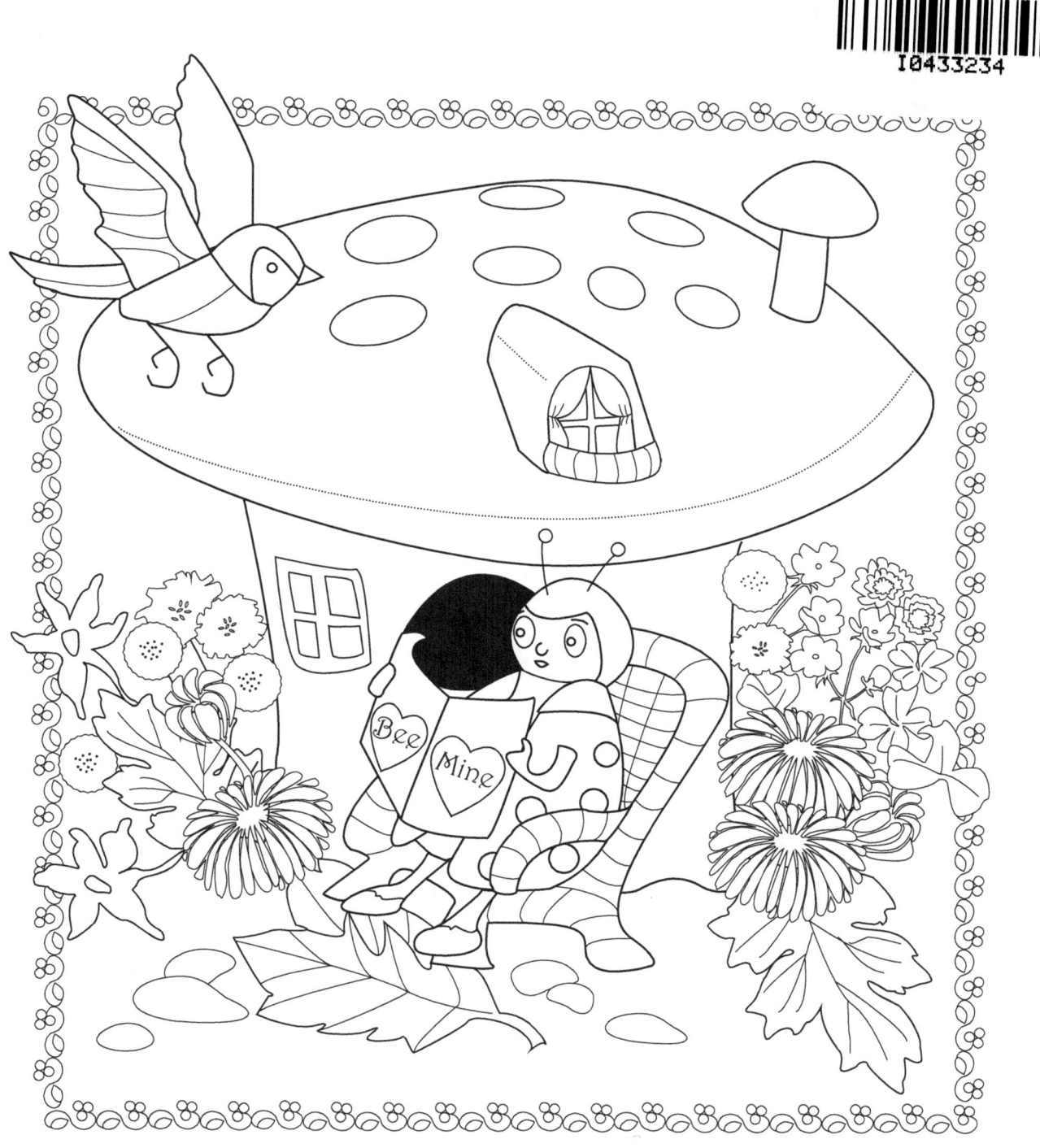

DonnaFreitag.com

How to color this book

I Colored This Picture For You is a coloring book for adults. You'll enjoy hours of creative, relaxing, stress relieving fun as you color 25 all new designs. All are beautiful, new, original artwork never before seen in any collection.

Coloring Tips

Colored pencils are the most popular way to color. It's best to get a large set of at least 48 colors. Some of the best brands are Prismacolor and Staedtler.

In addition, you'll need an eraser and a good pencil sharpener. Also popular are markers. Warning: they tend to bleed through the page. So if you use them, place a sheet or thick paper underneath so the ink doesn't leak onto the picture below. Copic markers are a great brand.

Marker sets offer a smaller choice of colors than pencil sets. That's one reason why the pro colorists often use a combination of pencils, markers, gel pens and even crayons.

It all depends on the effects you want to produce.

Please post photos of your artwork on my Facebook page. I'd love to see what you've done!

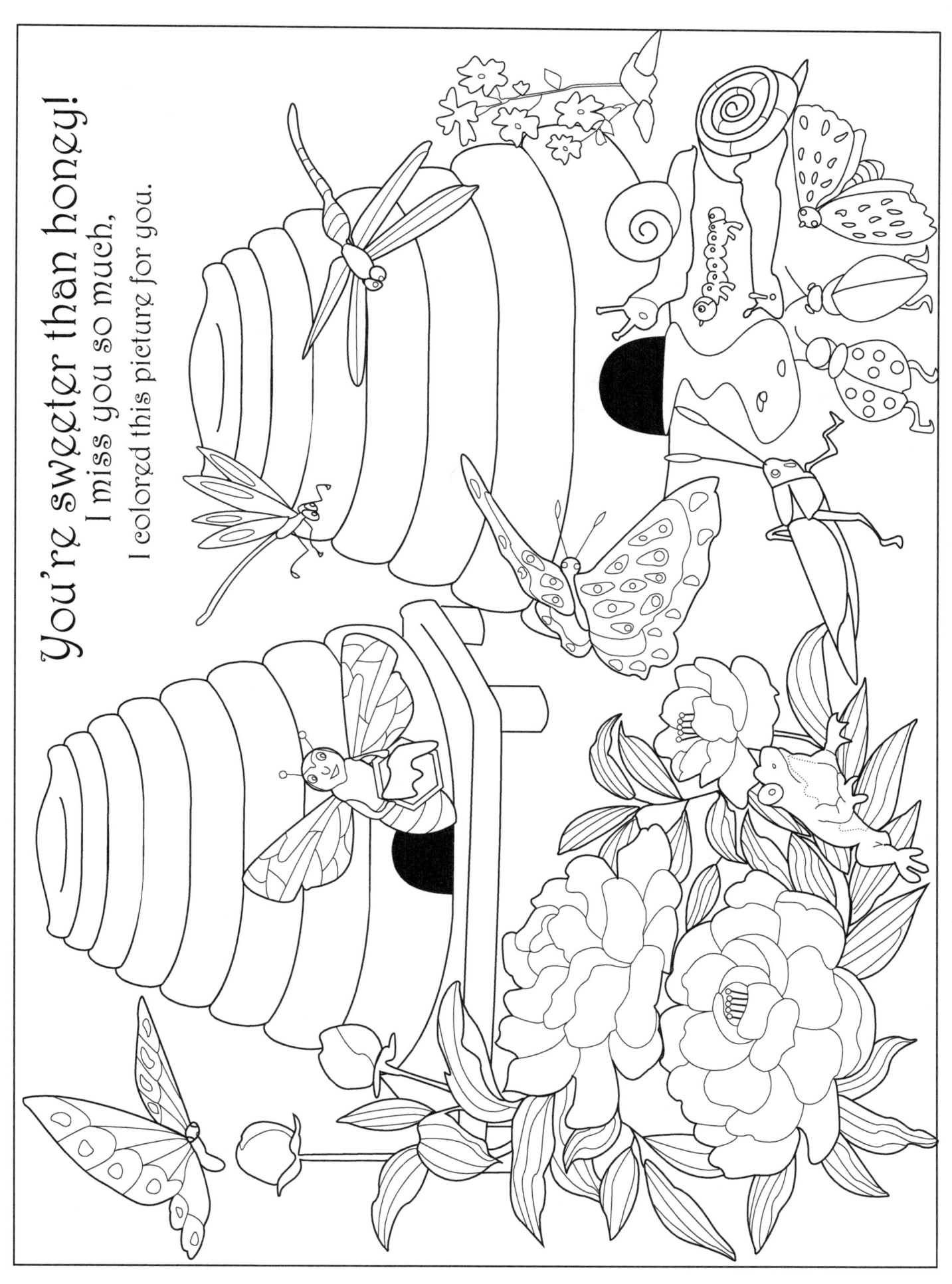

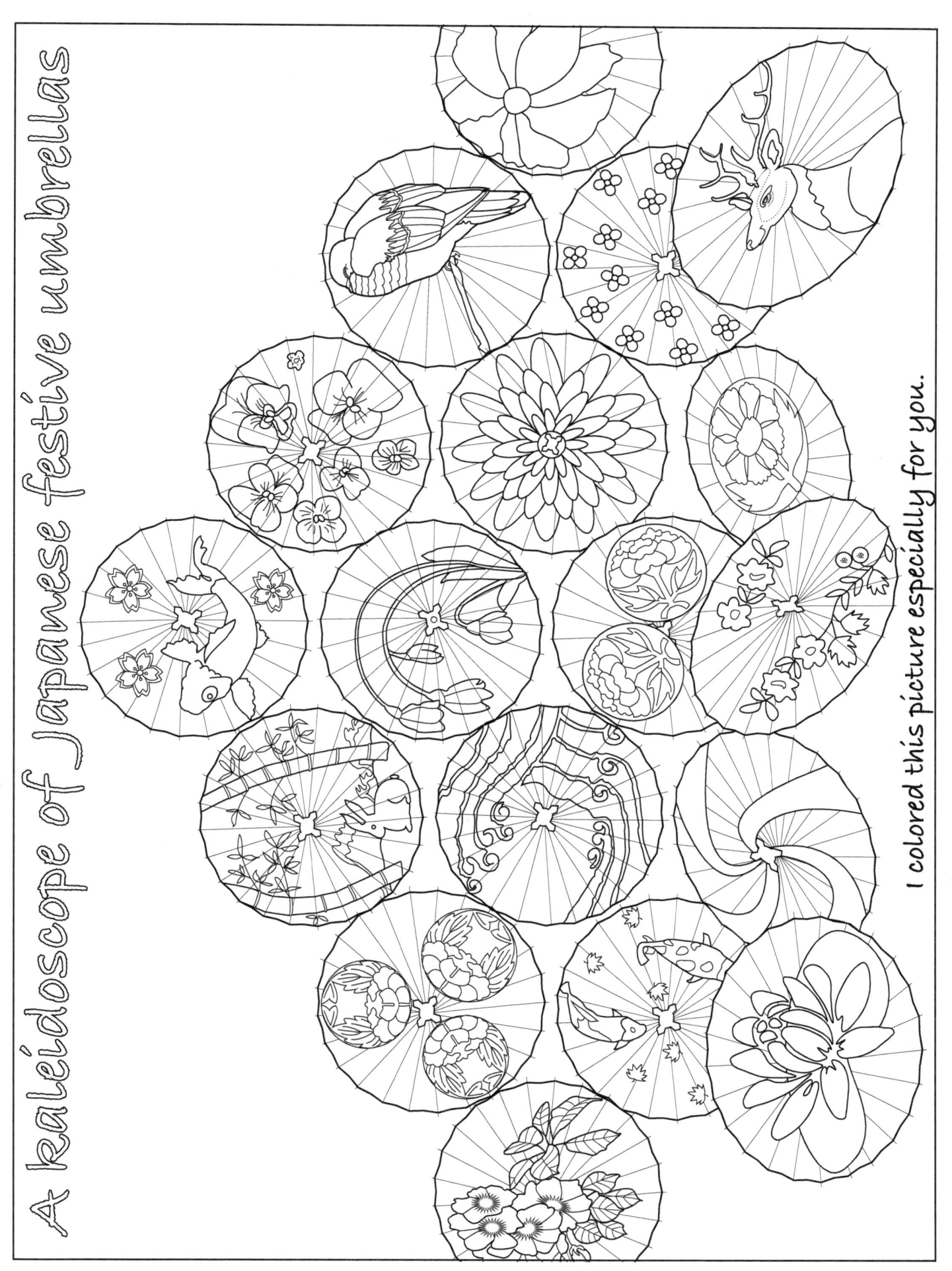

A kaleidoscope of Japanese festive umbrellas

I colored this picture especially for you.

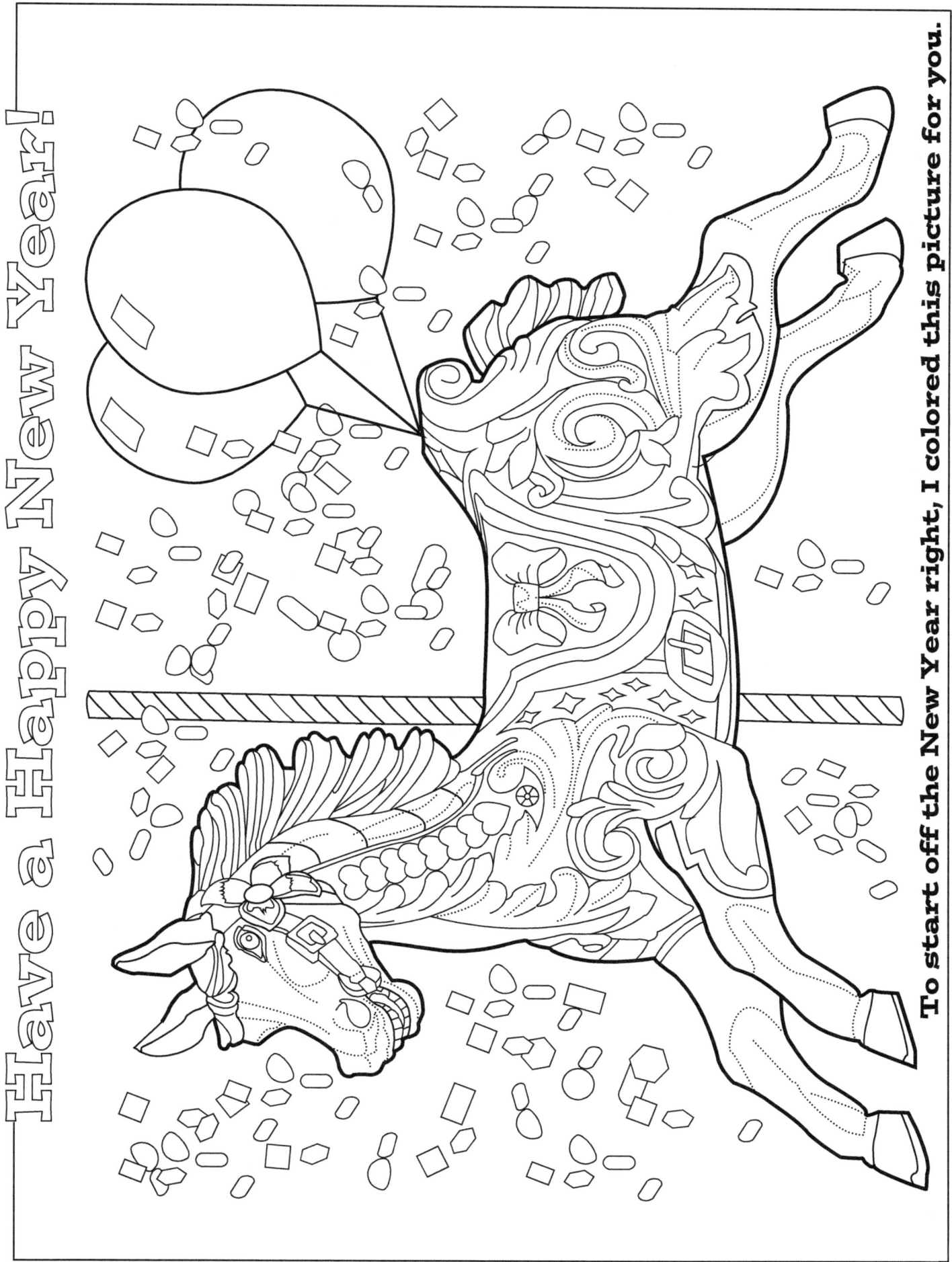

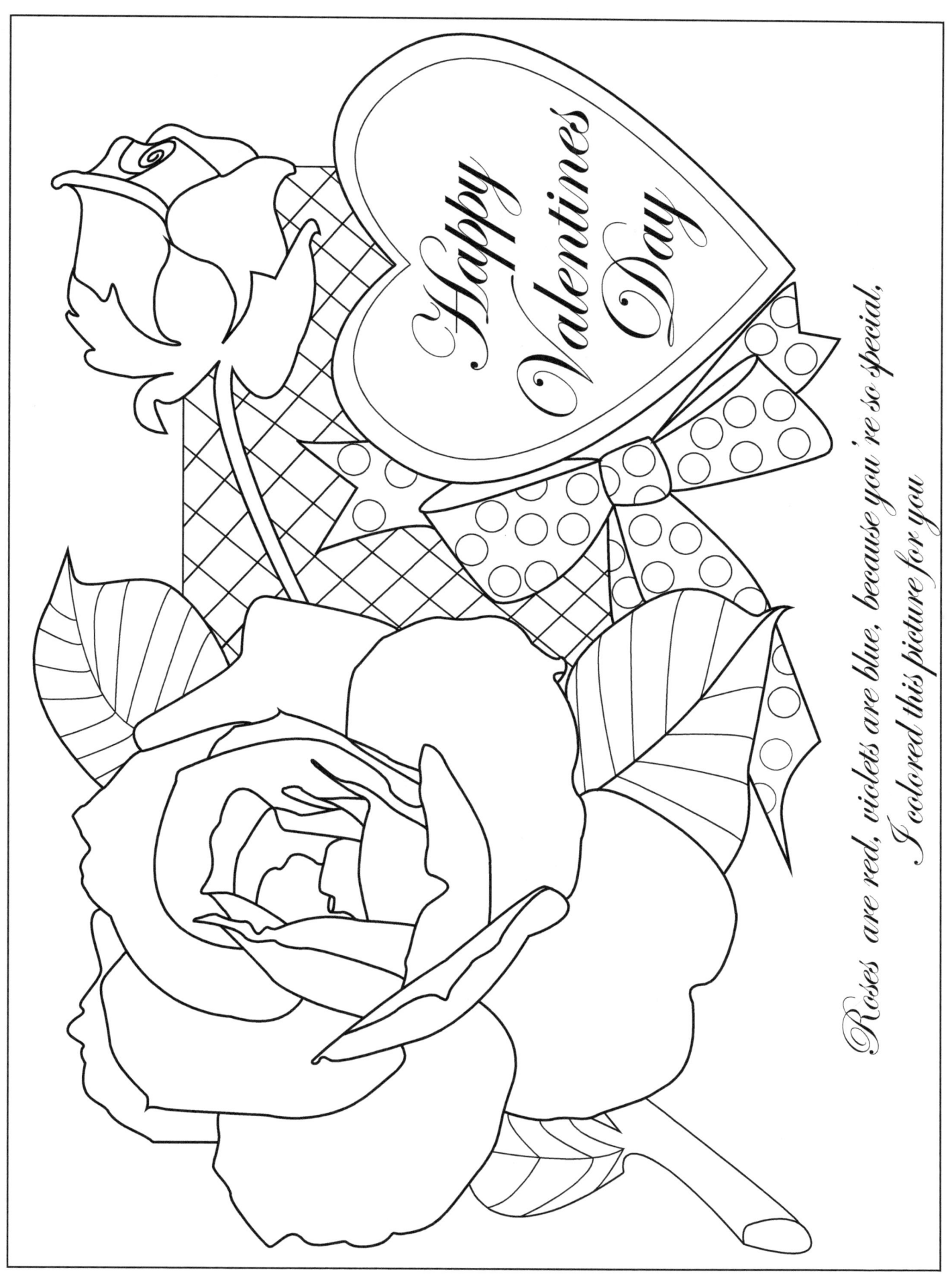

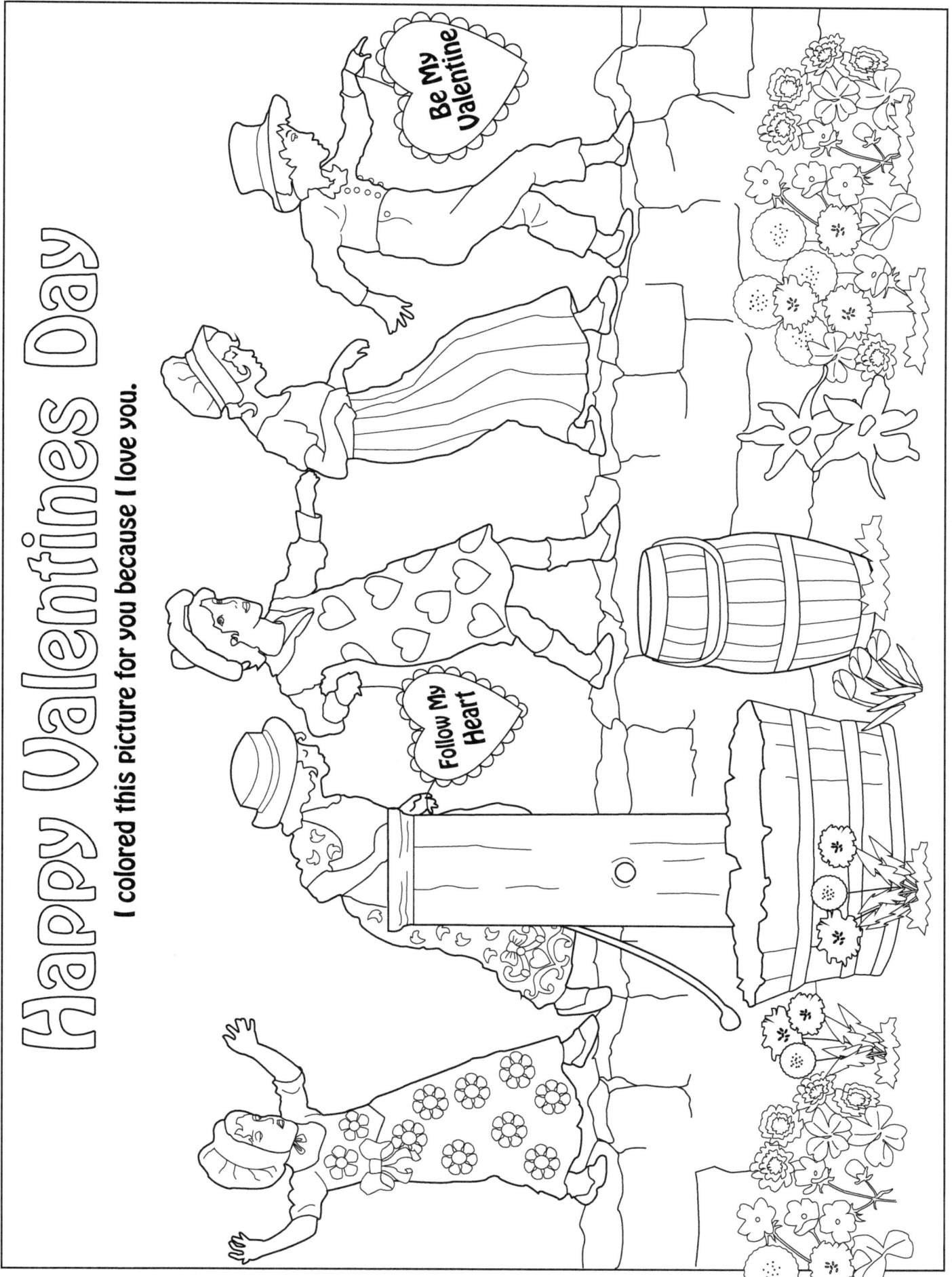

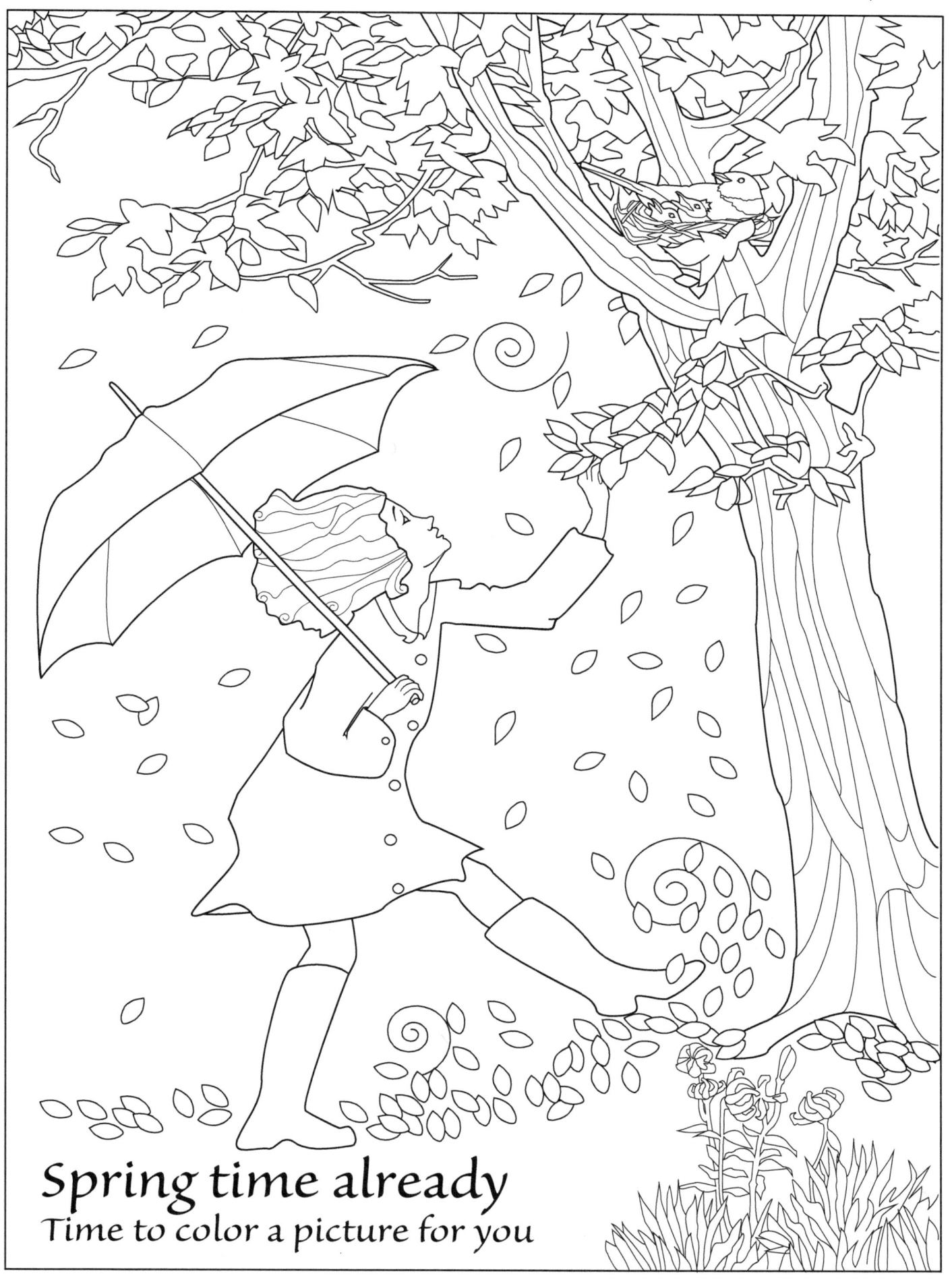

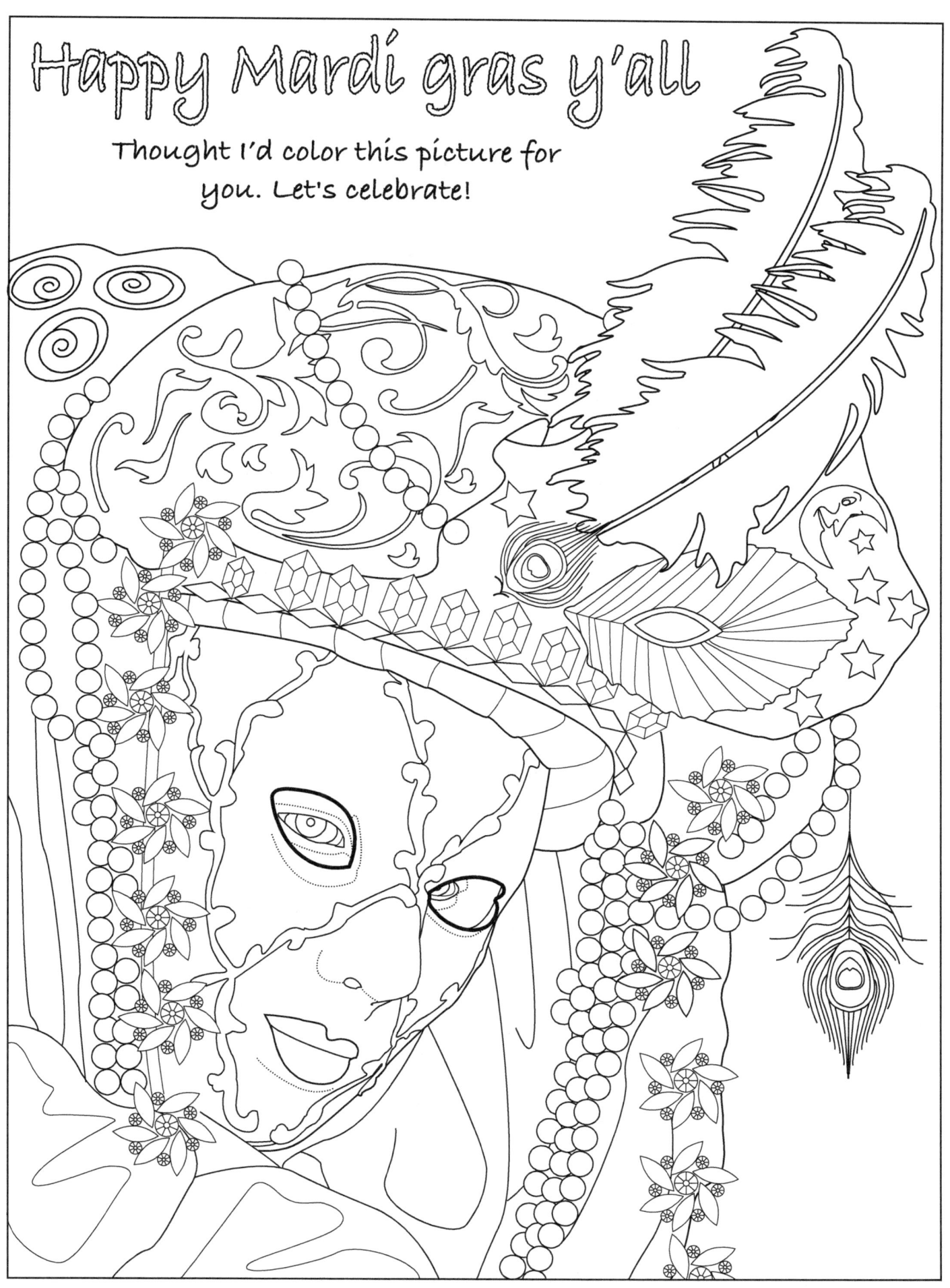

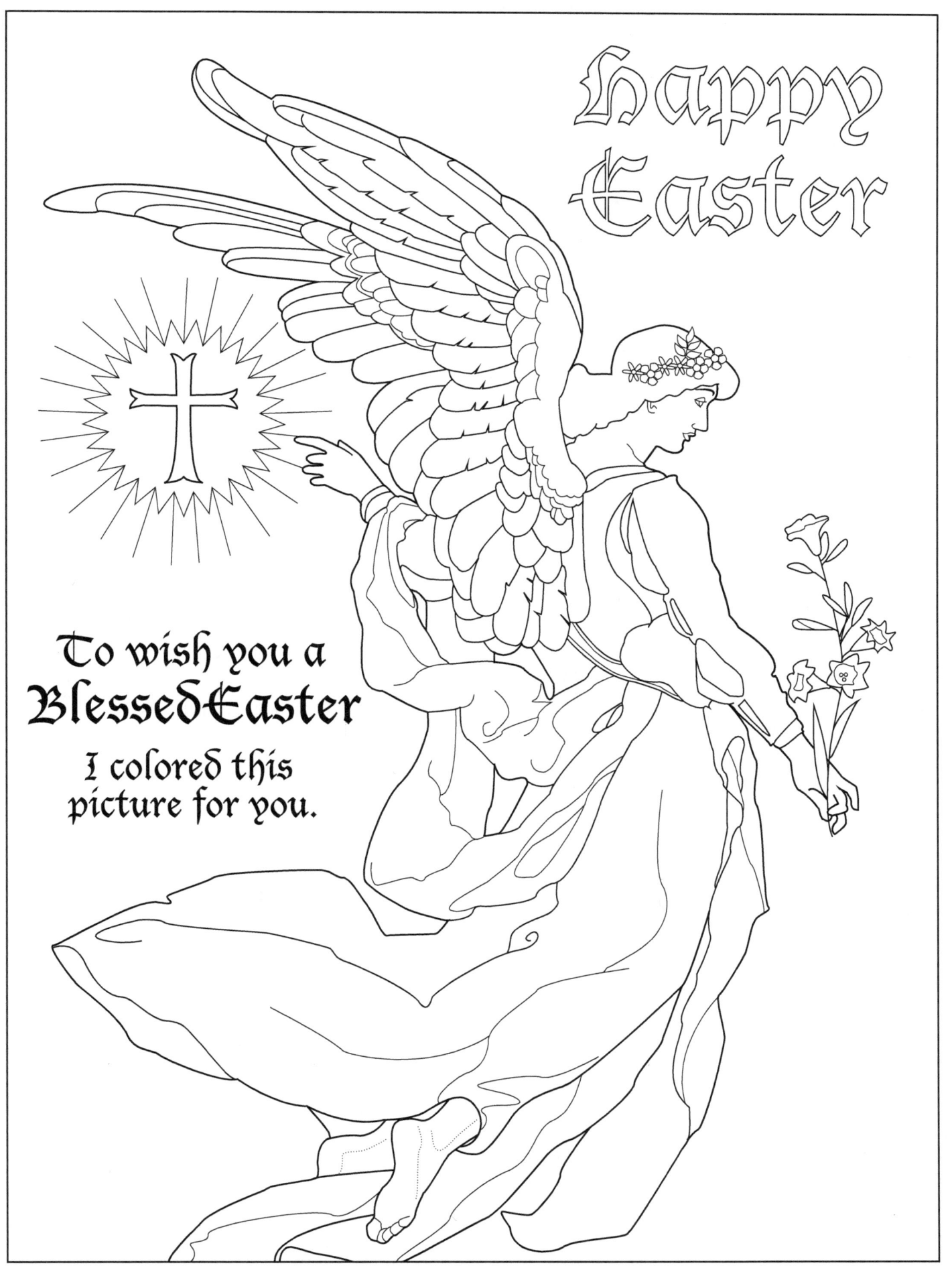

Happy Easter
I colored this picture for you

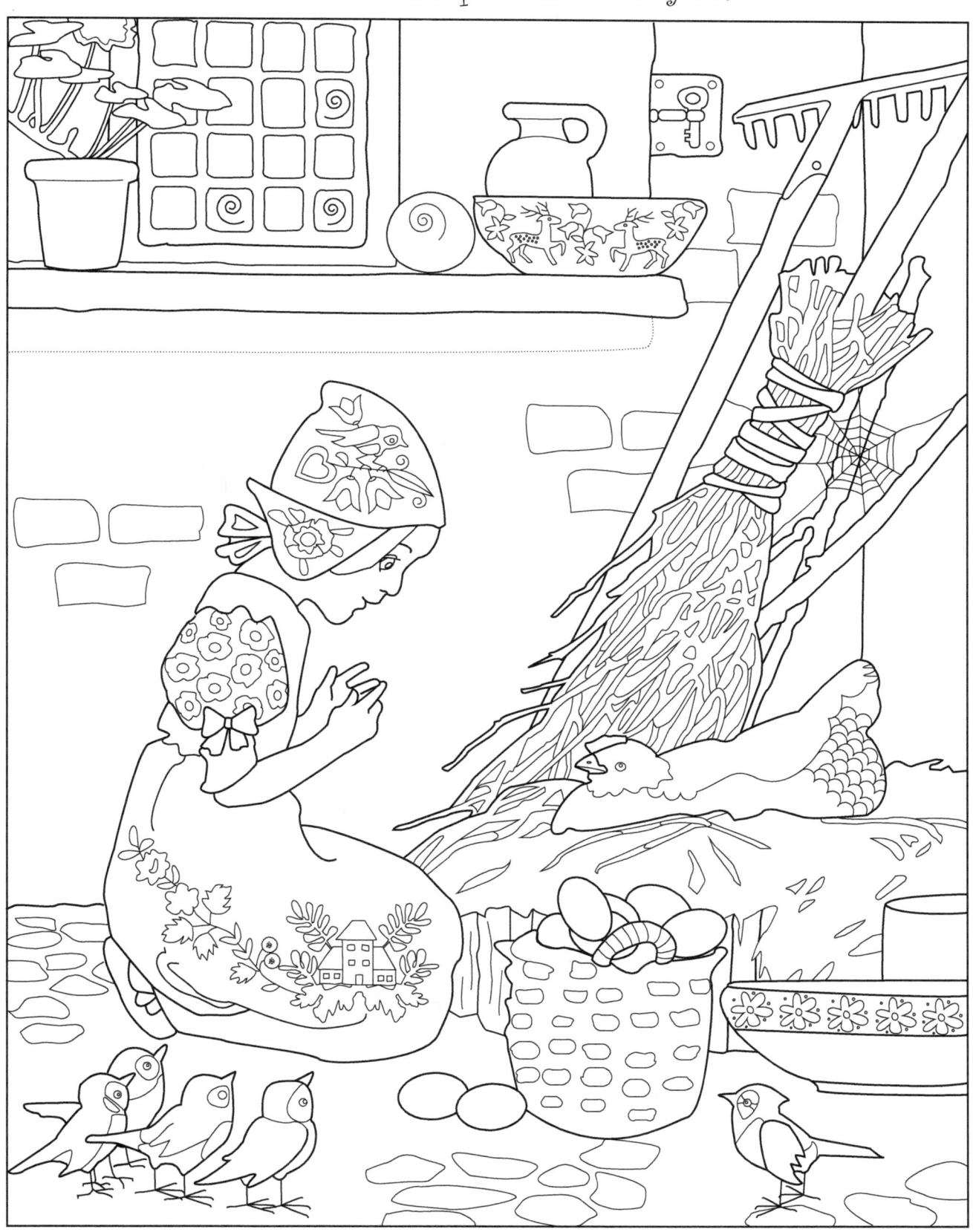

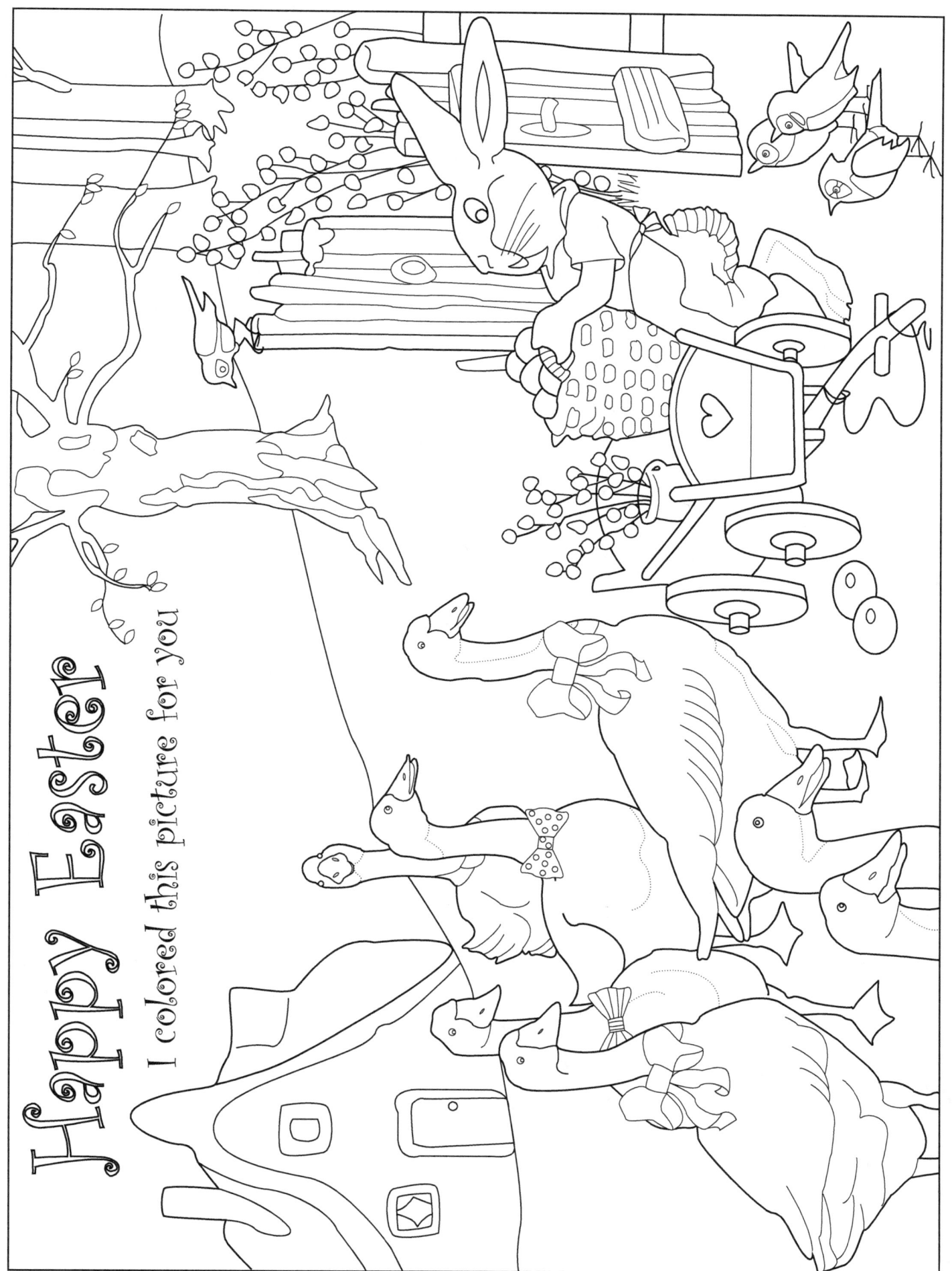

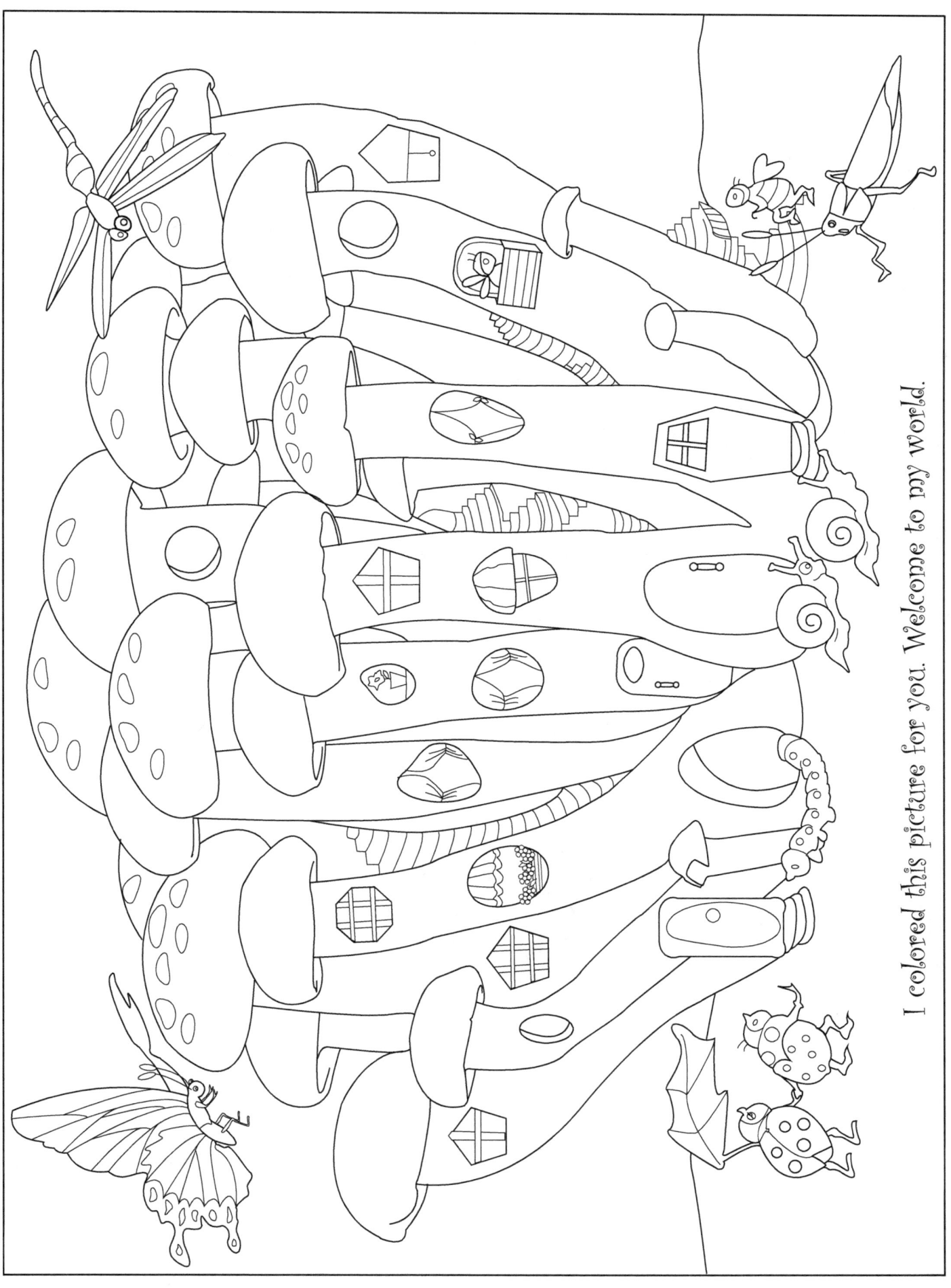

I colored this picture for you. Welcome to my world.

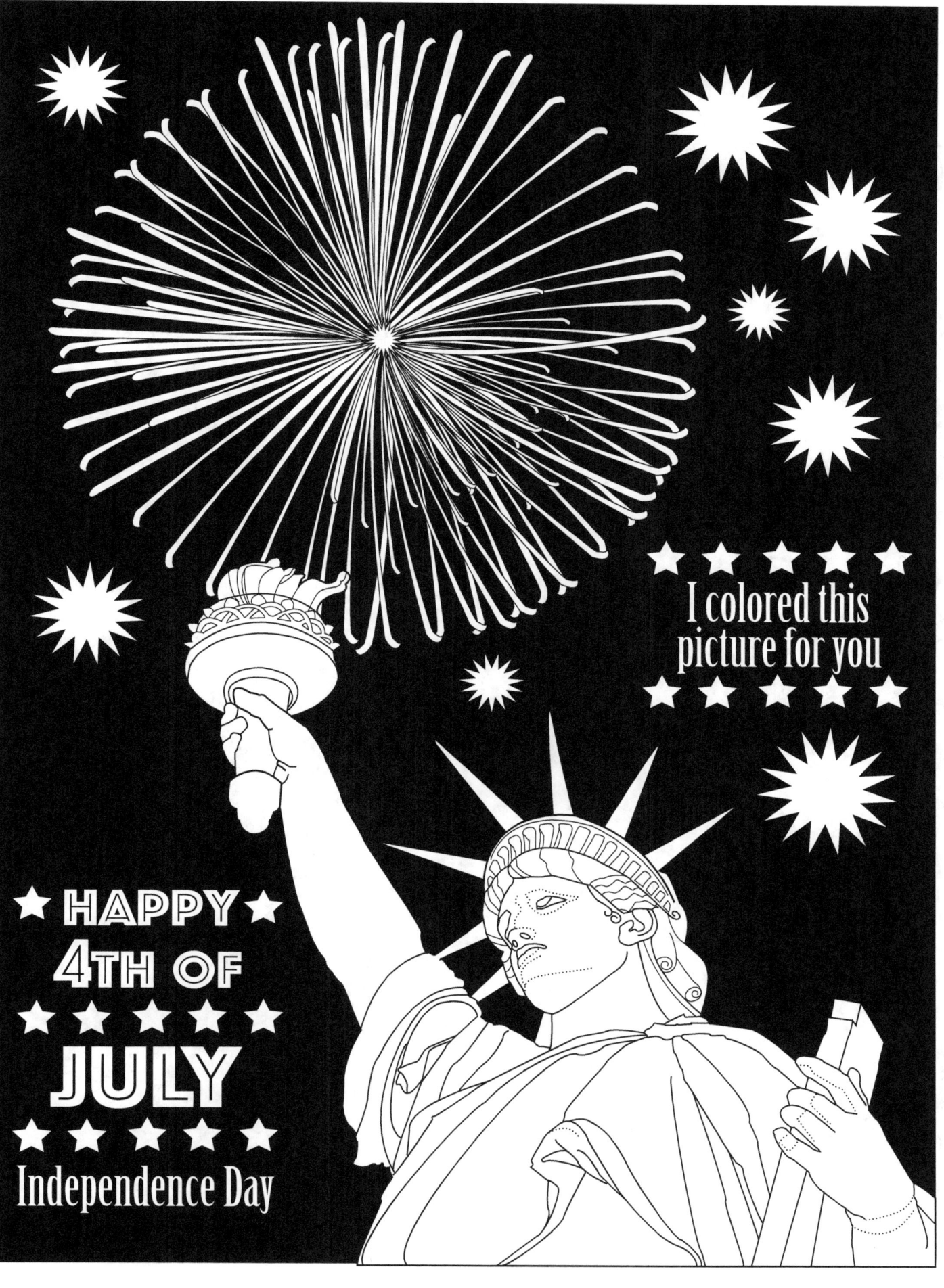

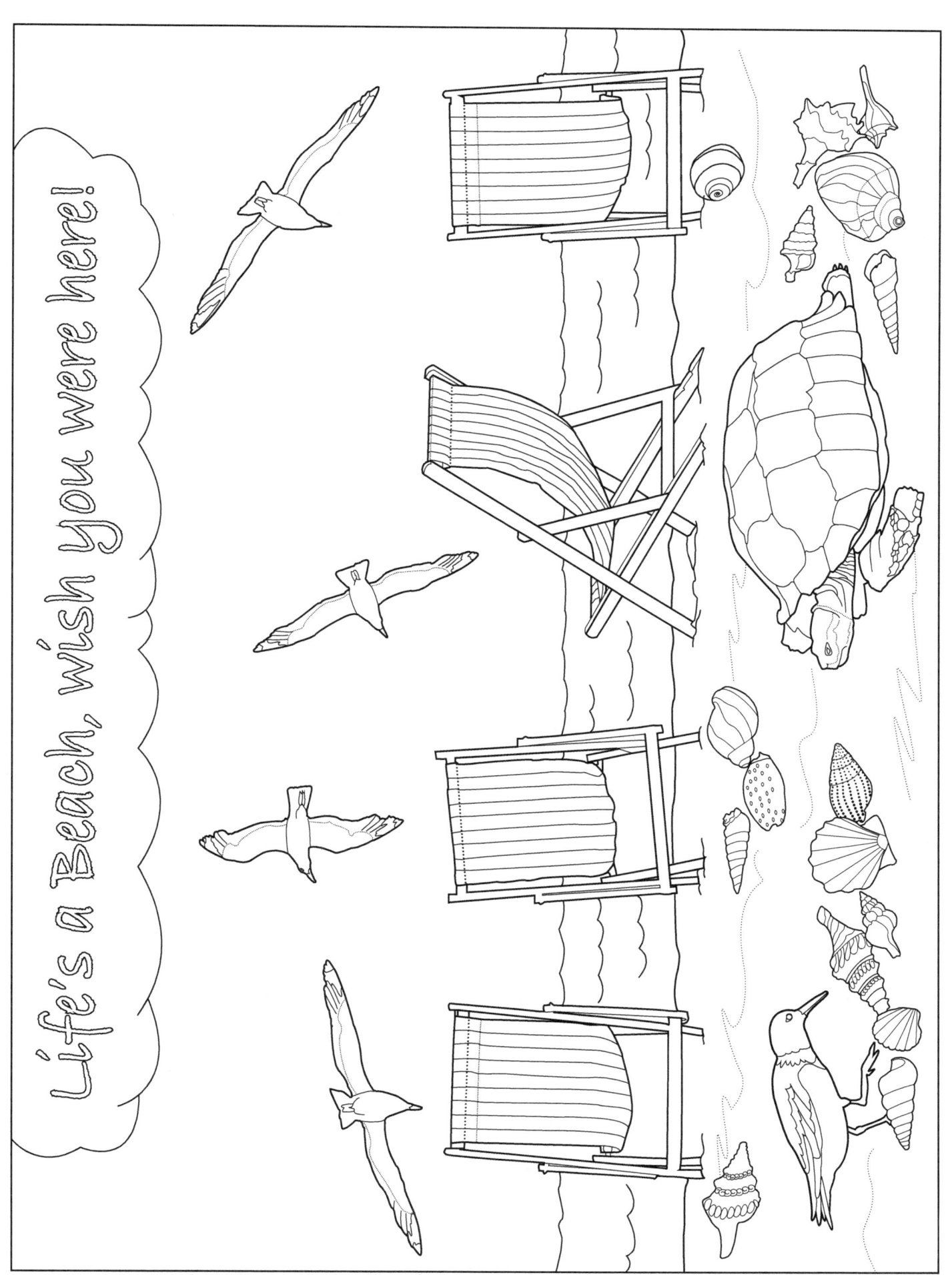

Tropical Greetings

This picture I colored for you is filled with warm & bright wishes.

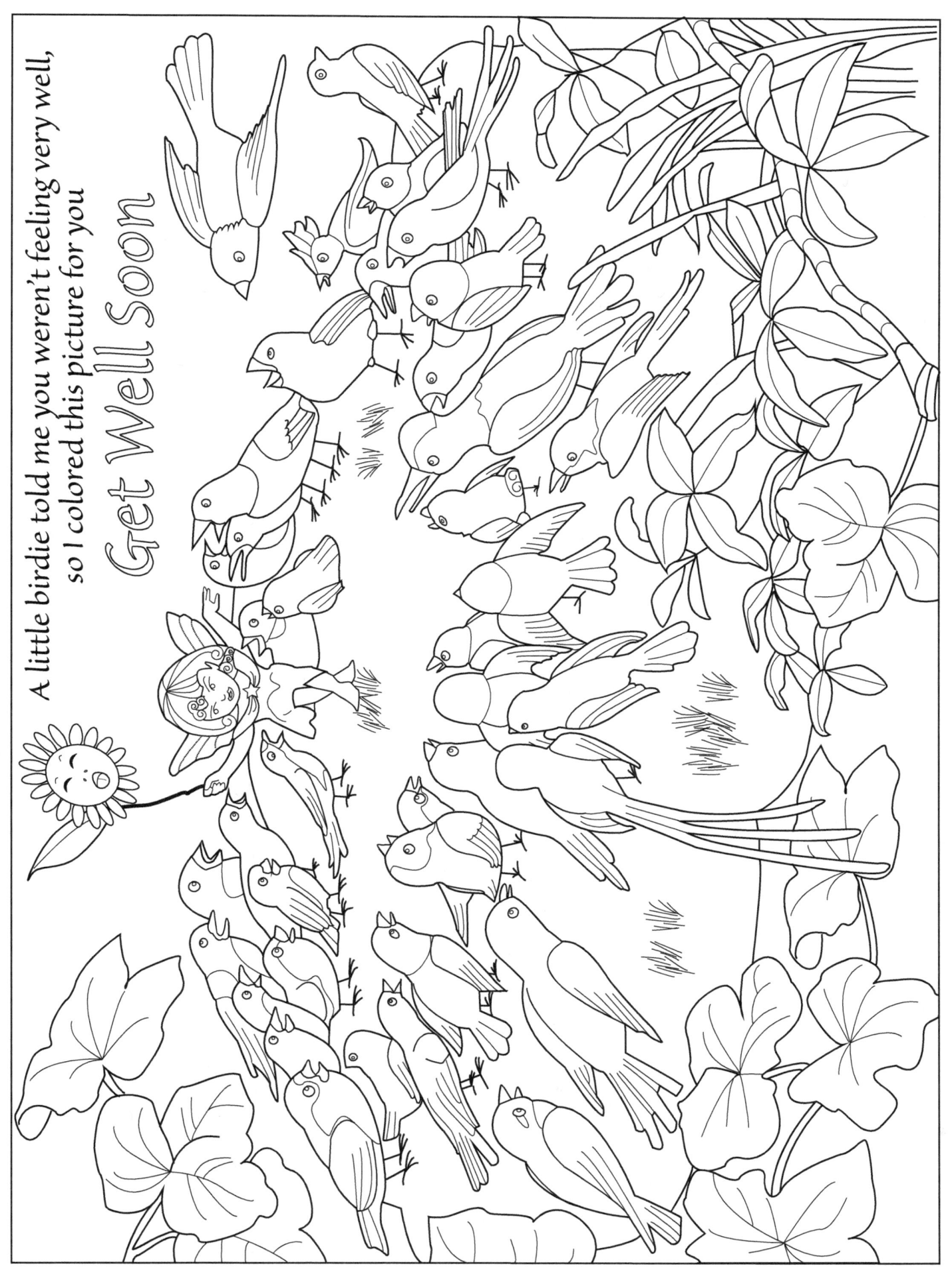

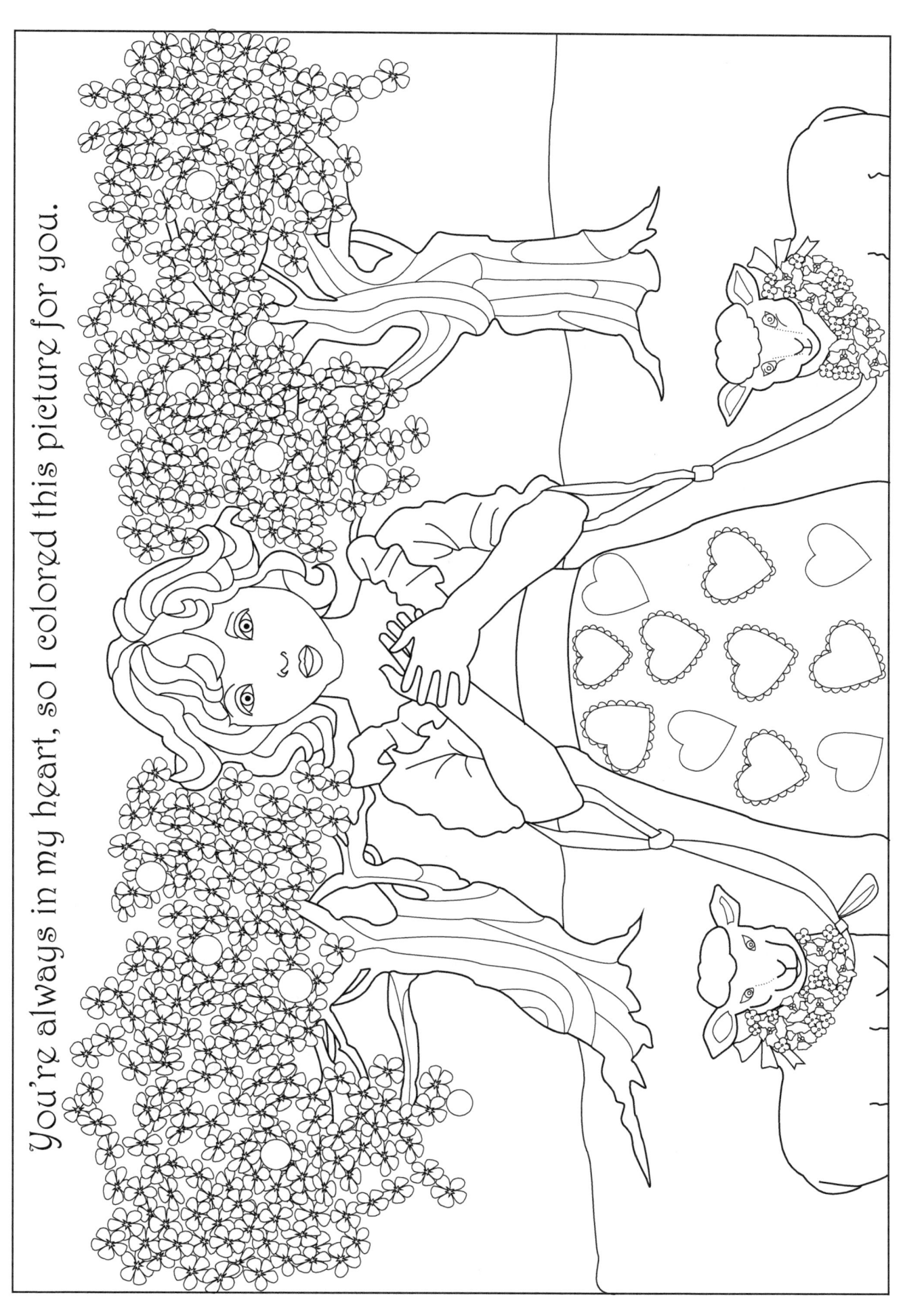

You're always in my heart, so I colored this picture for you.

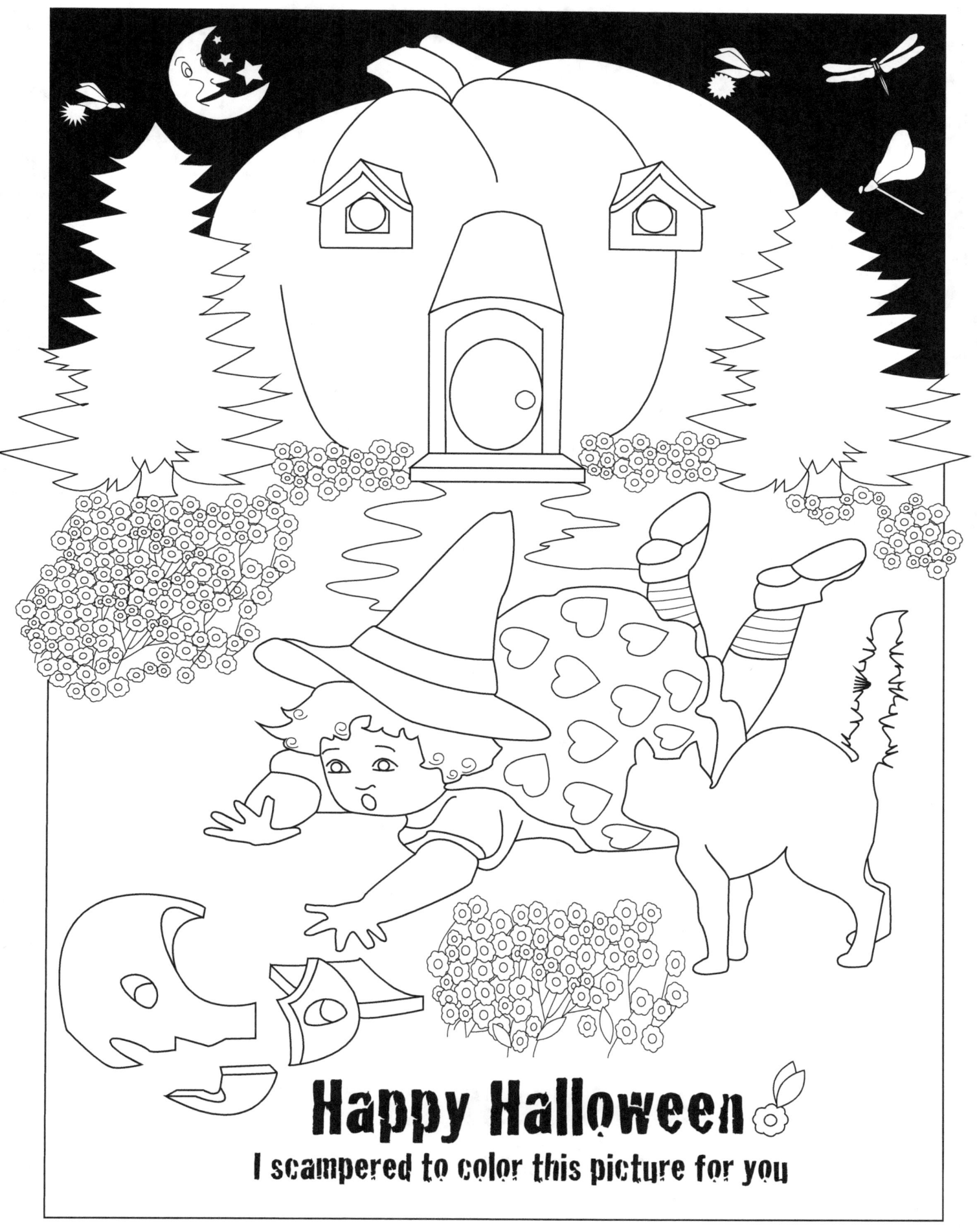

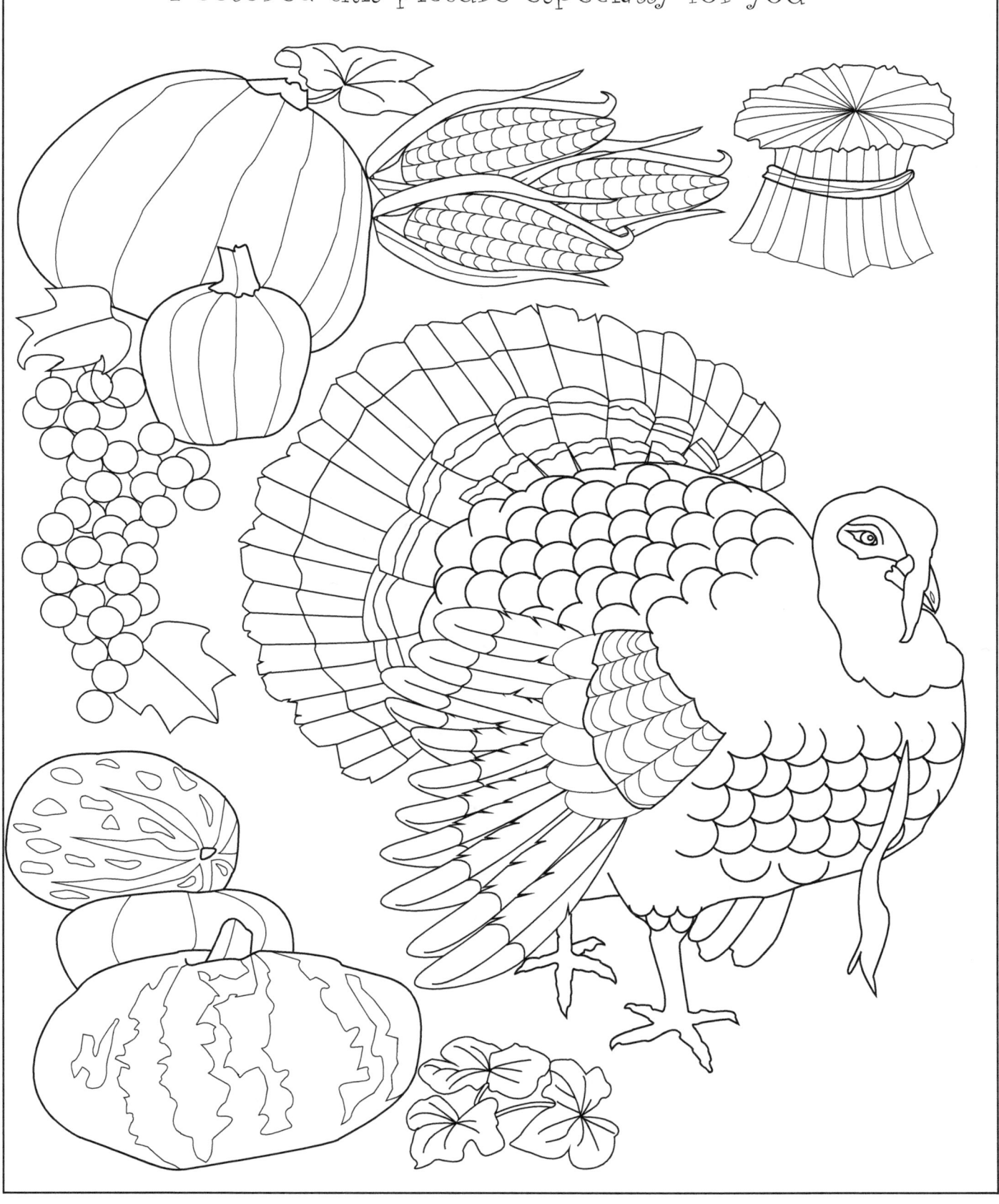

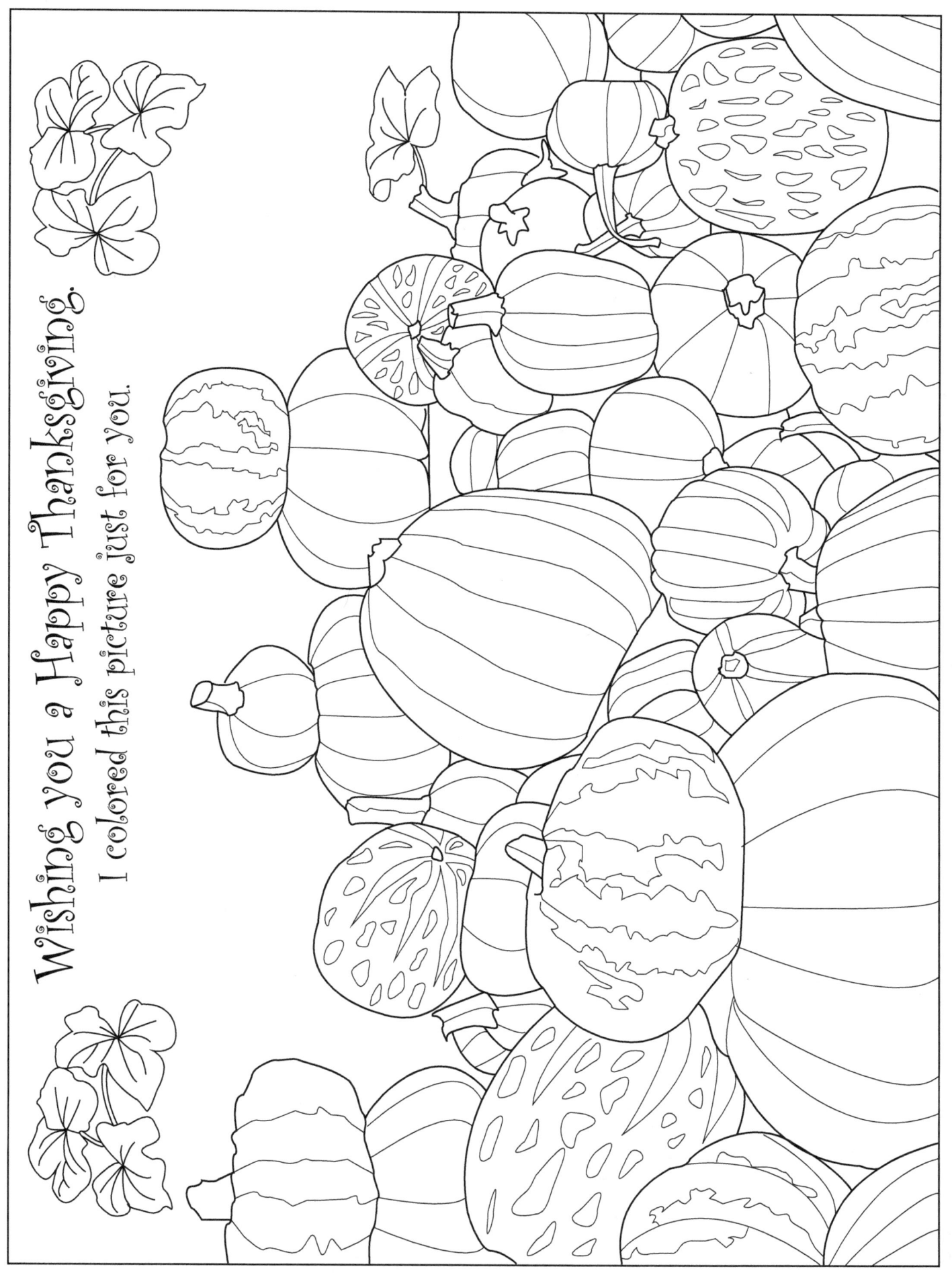

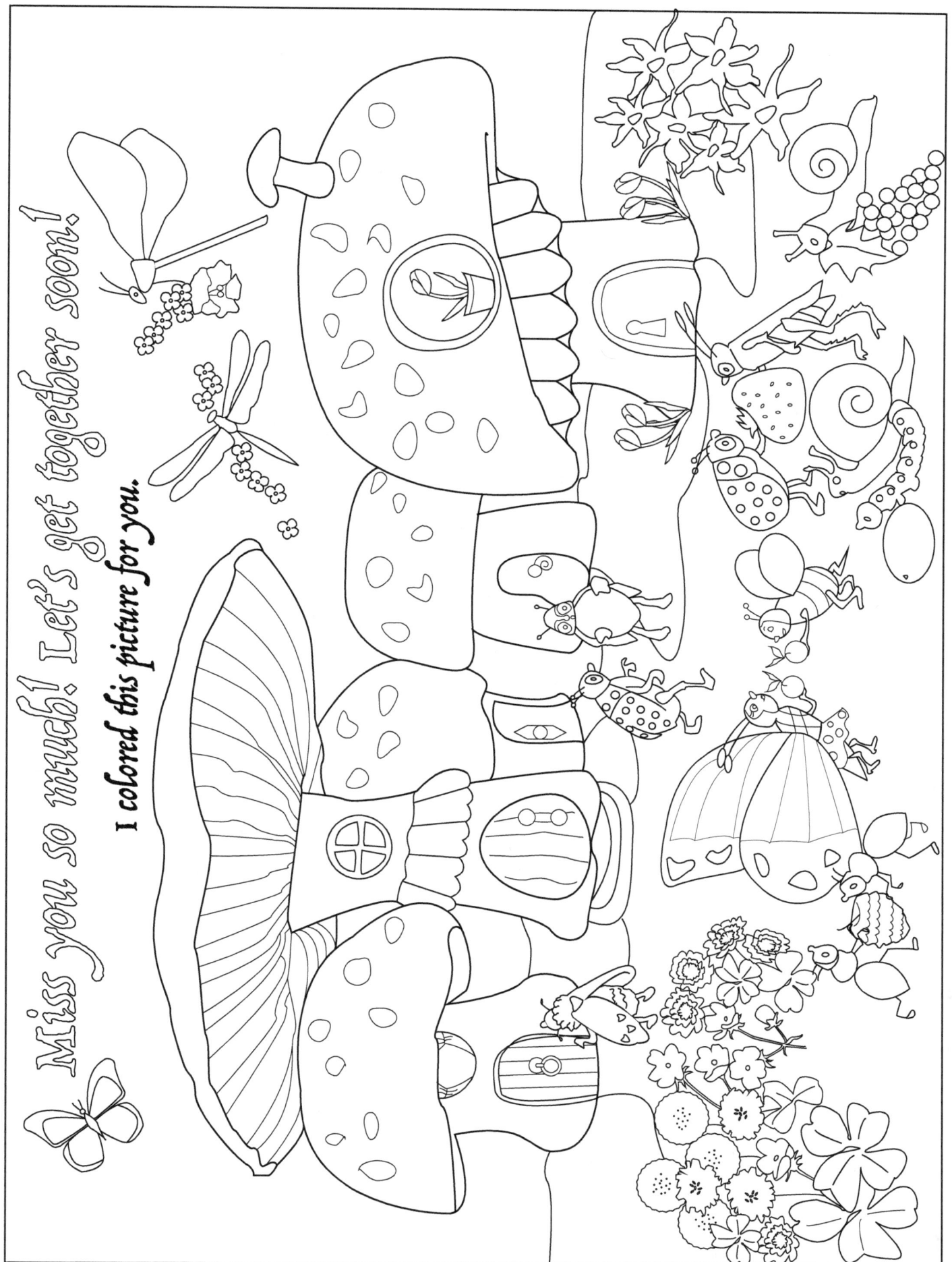

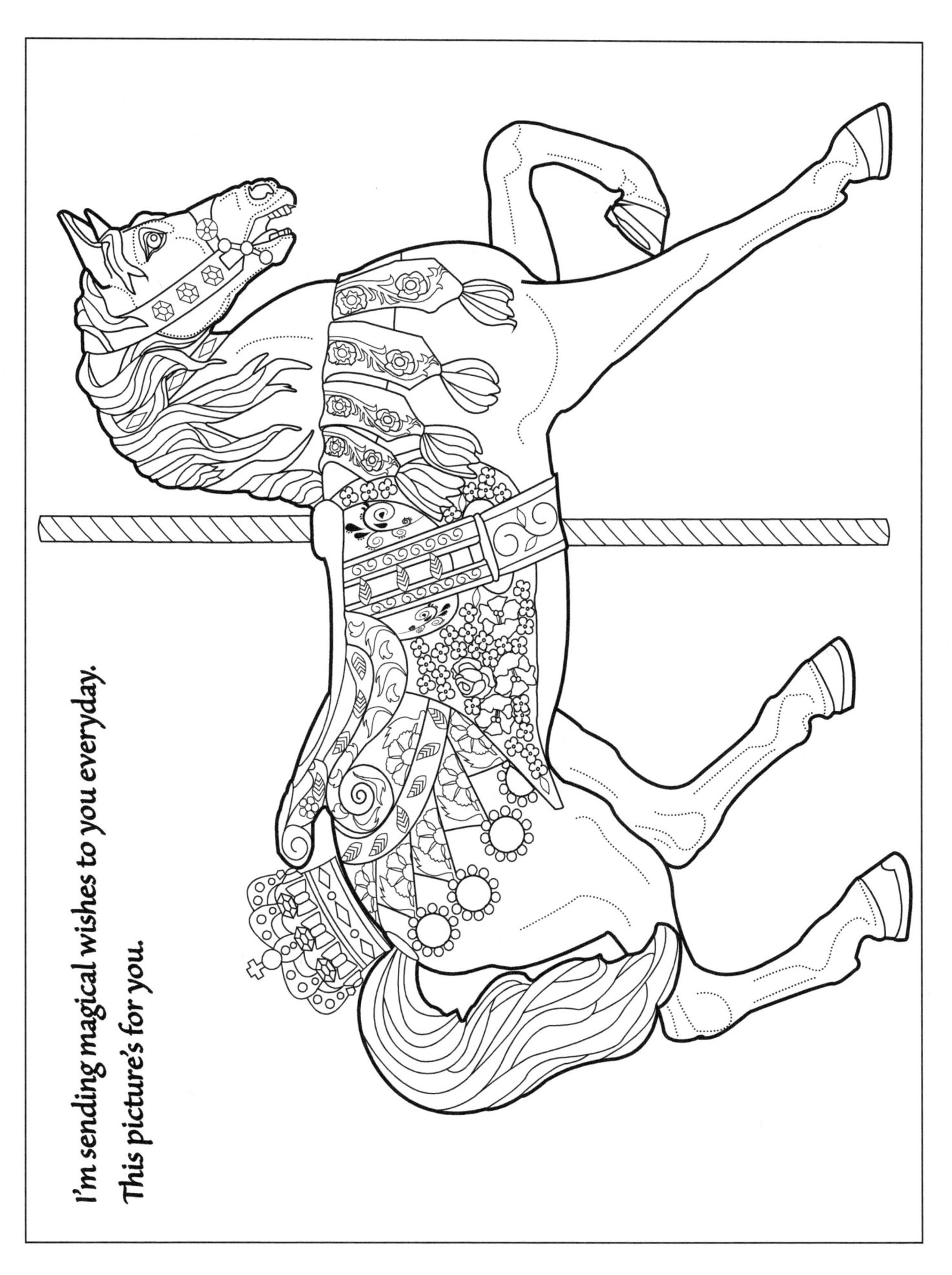

I'm sending magical wishes to you everyday.
This picture's for you.

Merry Christmas
Thinking of you during this holy season,
and colored this picture for you. Have a Blessed Christmas.

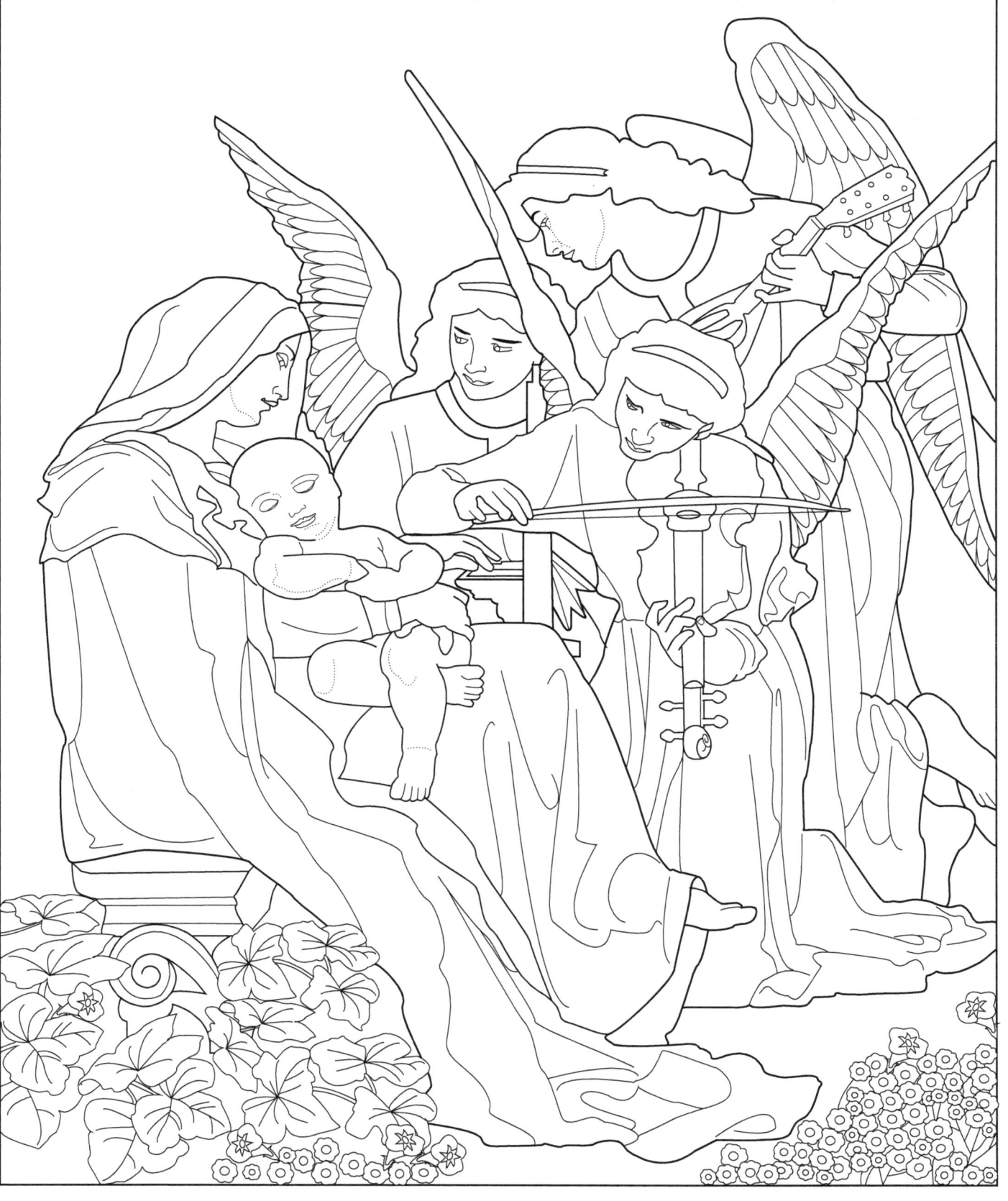

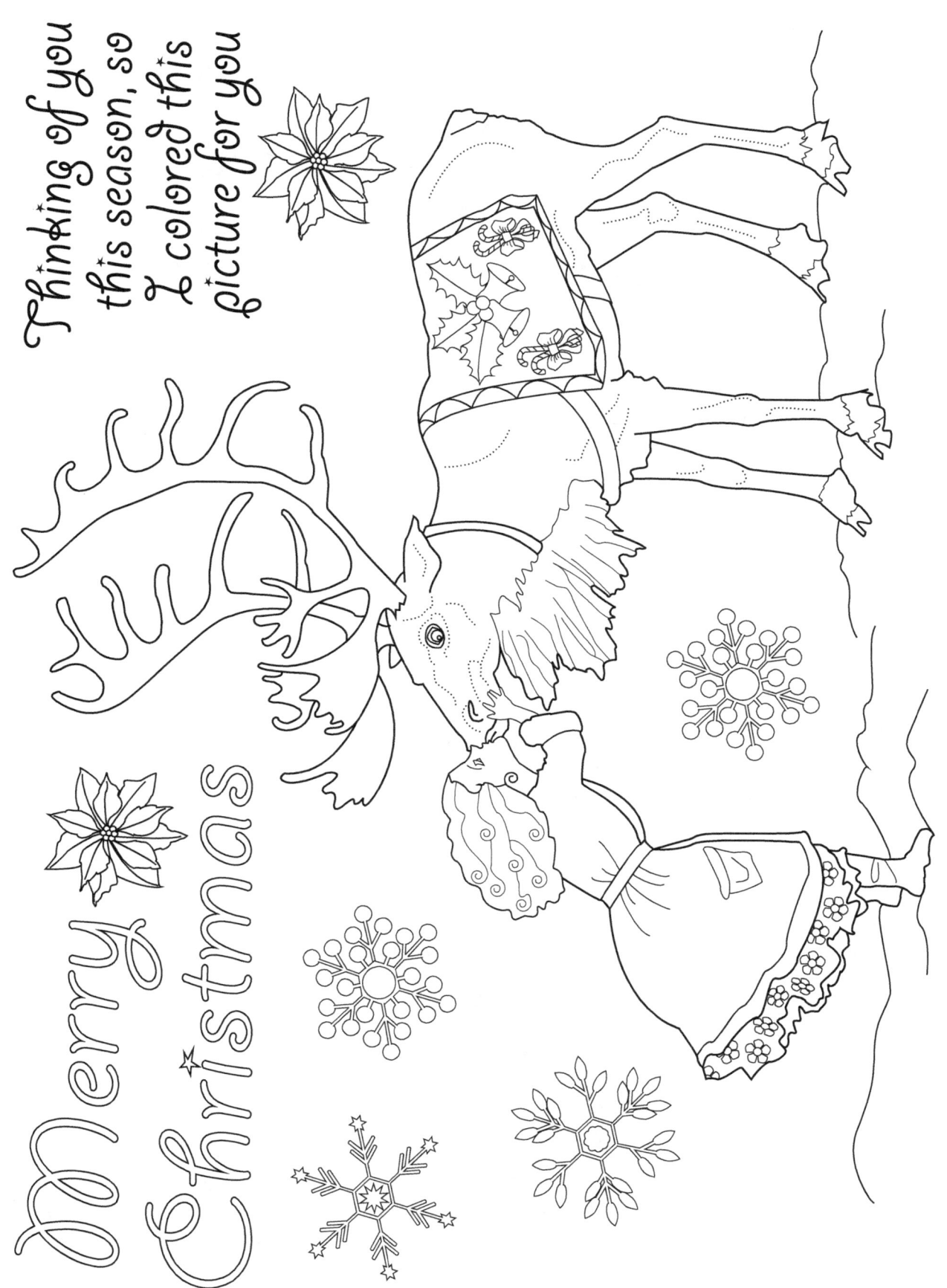

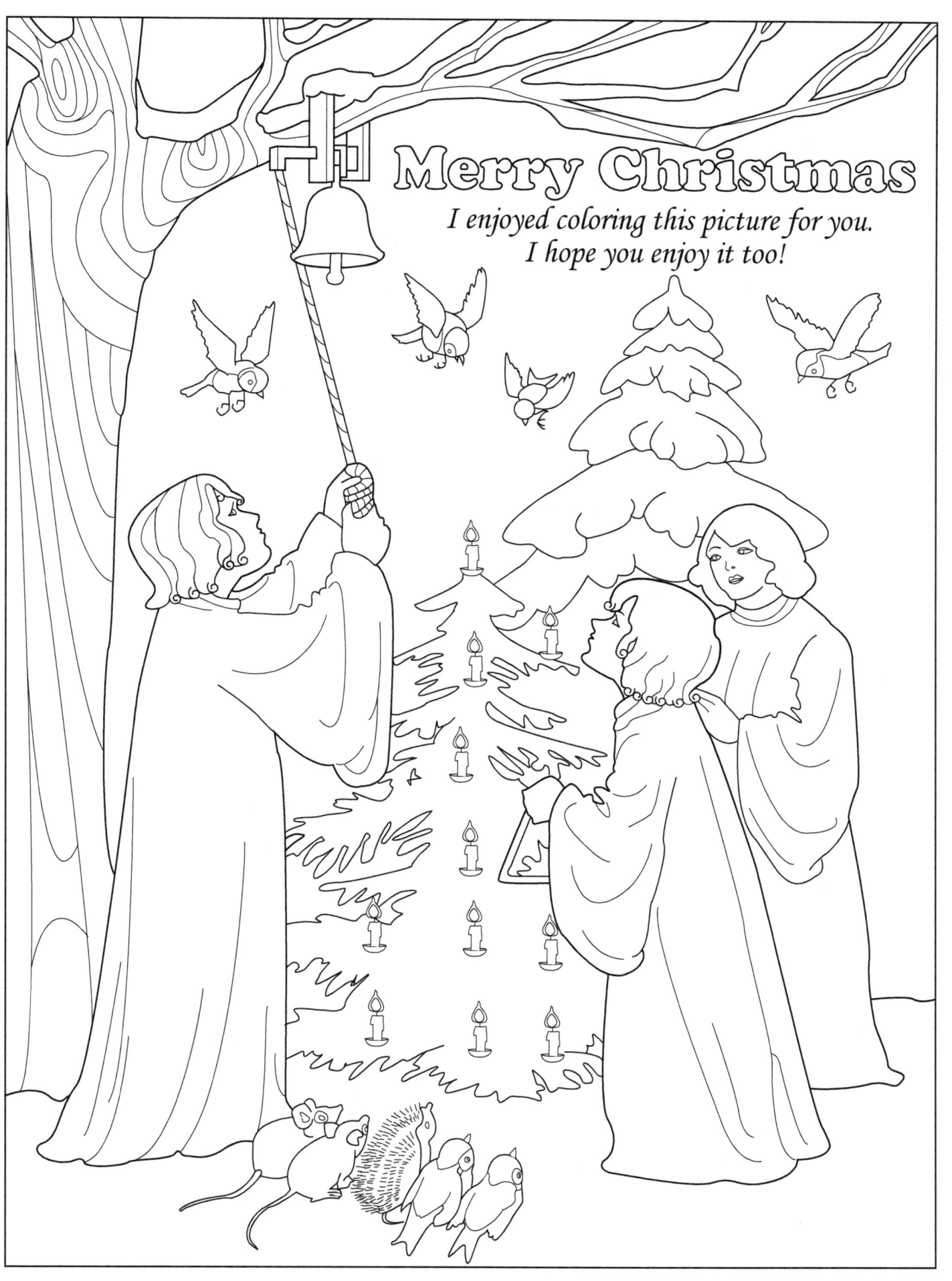

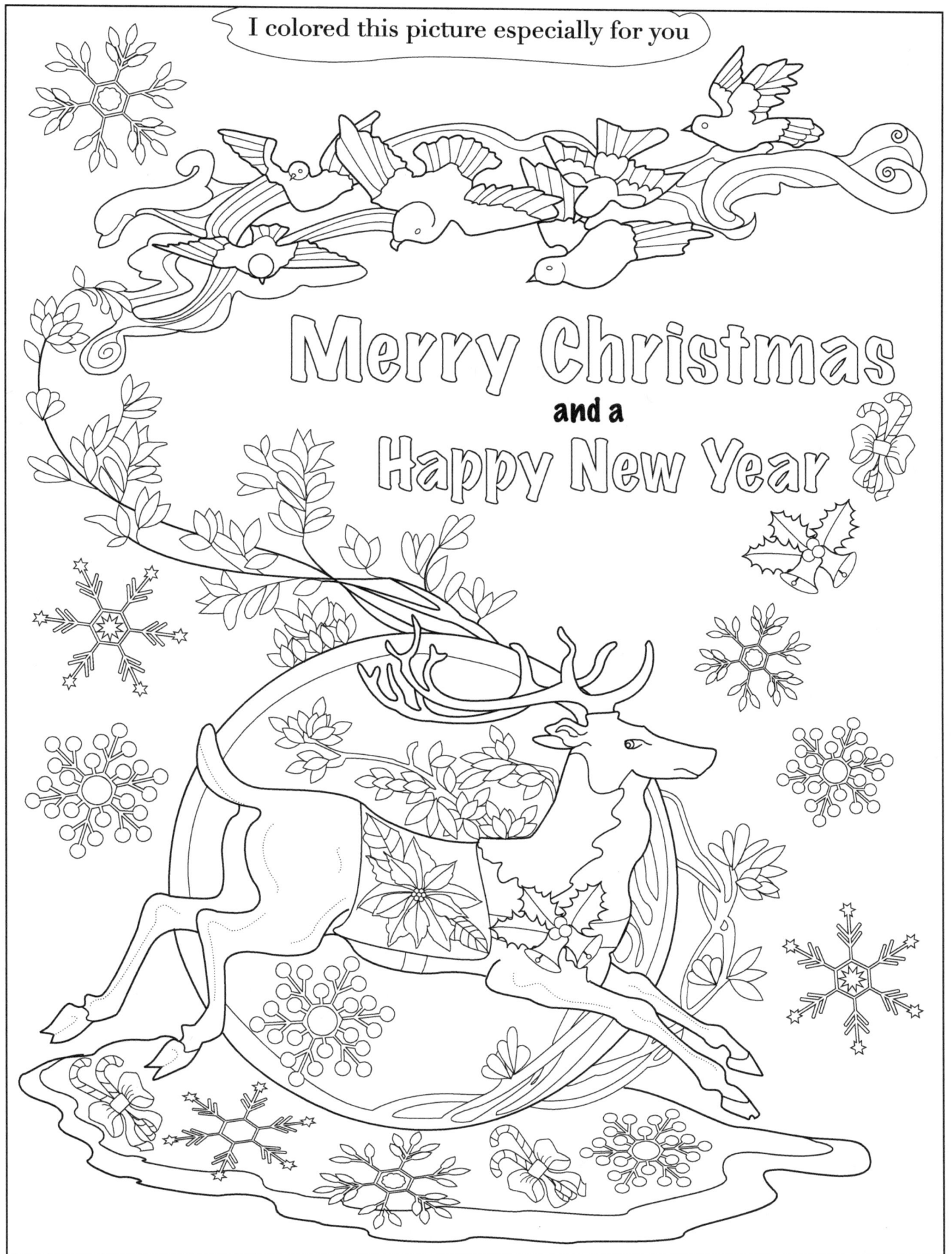

Be sure to follow us on social media...

f donnafreitag90

t @donna_r_freitag

i @donnafreitag1991

p donna_freitag

Join our mailing list for the latest news and freebies.

Visit www.donnafreitag.com

www.ingramcontent.com/pod-product-compliance
Lightning Source LLC
Chambersburg PA
CBHW062201220526
45470CB00009B/2889